I AM
STRONGER THAN...

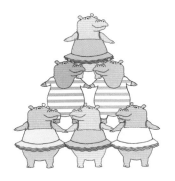

Published and distributed by Knock Knock
6080 Center Drive
Los Angeles, CA 90045
knockknockstuff.com
Knock Knock is a registered trademark of Knock Knock LLC
Affirmators! is a registered trademark of Knock Knock LLC

© 2018 Suzi Barrett
Illustrations by Naomi Sloman
Illustrations © 2018 Knock Knock LLC
All rights reserved
Printed in China

ISBN: 978-168349109-5
UPC: 825703-50183-4

10 9 8 7 6 5 4 3

I AM
STRONGER THAN…

**Affirmators!® to Remind You
You're Stronger Than
Just About Anything**

Suzi Barrett

**KNOCK
KNOCK®**
LOS ANGELES, CALIFORNIA

The key to any positive affirmation is to say it with **conviction**.* The problem is, it's not always easy to feel convincingly confident—especially when life is bullying you with the bad days. For that reason, this book is organized on a scale from 1 to 60, with the easiest to believe Affirmators! in the front of the book, and the much more advanced Affirmators! towards the end.

You can start at the beginning if you need an extra dose of strength, or just flip around. It's up to you.

*See how we did that?

**I am stronger
than bent wheat.**

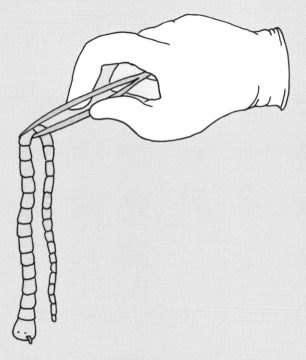

I am stronger than
a flaccid tapeworm.

I am stronger
than wet yarn.

I am stronger than
houses built of
scrambled eggs.

I am stronger than every contender in the flea Olympics.

I am stronger than the
faint whiff of clam.

I am stronger than anyone's opinions on Luxembourg.

I am stronger than
the emotional
baggage of a freshly
divorced goldfish.

I am stronger than the
sentimentality inspired
by a greeting card.

I am stronger than
the reigning red rover
champs of Rumford,
Rhode Island.

I am stronger than that
drowning mosquito's
dog paddle.

I am stronger than
a squash that hasn't
been squashed.

I am stronger than
a simple concrete
foundation.

I am stronger than the thrust of a legal-everywhere, sold-in-grocery-stores bottle rocket.

I am stronger than an underwater phone signal.

I am stronger than
a rom-com couple's
chemistry.

I am stronger than a brisk, southeasterly wind.

I am stronger than a retired kitten boxer.

I am stronger than a lobster with a gym membership.

I am stronger than a ghost's desire to see who is sleeping in his former bedroom.

I am stronger than that young valet's cologne.

I am stronger than
the persistence of
a glacier.

I am stronger than most conspiracy theorists' logic.

I am stronger than a
pyramid of hippos.

I am stronger than
an undefeated arm-
wrestler, offended.

I am stronger than
drunk ogre breath.

I am stronger than anyone whose nickname contains the word "rock."

I am stronger than gravity on Jupiter.

I am stronger than Al Capone's "usual."

I am stronger
than a guerrilla
graffiti artist's
street cred.

I am stronger than the
inevitability of time.

I am stronger
than a trapeze
artist's grip.

I am stronger than
President Dinosaur's
handshake.

I am stronger than the
all-pervasive vapor of
rotting Gouda.

I am stronger
than a shark
with a vendetta.

I am stronger than a preschooler's argument against bedtime.

I am stronger than
my reflection's
resemblance to me.

I am stronger than a
diamond-tipped juggernaut.

I am stronger than
a parent's wishes
for their newborn's
unfolding life.

I am stronger than
dictator hyperbole.

I am stronger than three parts vinegar, one part straight-up acid.

I am stronger than
a fortress of safes.

I am stronger than one of those families that's the subject of a heartwarming "based on true events" movie.

I am stronger than a
trebuchet's tennis serve.

I am stronger than a kraken's desire to tear innocent sailors limb from limb.

I am stronger than two and a half abominable snowmen.

I am stronger
than strychnine.

I am stronger than my
best friend's clout.

I am stronger than a middle-school crush.

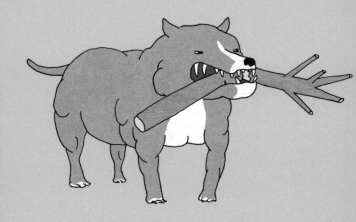

I am stronger than a
genetically modified
pit bull's jaws.

I am stronger than the Brawny paper towel guy, when he was in his prime. (Like, just-out-of-college Brawny paper towel guy.)

I am stronger than an
army of mastodons.

I am stronger than Mahler's kettledrums.

I am stronger than
our collective agreement
that heroin is not great
for your health.

I am stronger than
mutual disdain.

I am stronger than a
lottery winner's gratitude.

I am stronger than the taste
of that one raw onion that
found its way into my salad.

I am stronger
than PTA wrath.

I am
stronger than
Tank-zilla.

I am stronger than
my need to finish
this senten—